WHAT CANNOT BE FIXED

The Poiema Poetry Series

Poems are windows into worlds; windows into beauty, goodness, and truth; windows into understandings that won't twist themselves into tidy dogmatic statements; windows into experiences. We can do more than merely peer into such windows; with a little effort we can fling open the casements, and leap over the sills into the heart of these worlds. We are also led into familiar places of hurt, confusion, and disappointment, but we arrive in the poet's company. Poetry is a partnership between poet and reader, seeking together to gain something of value—to get at something important.

Ephesians 2:10 says, "We are God's workmanship..." *poiema* in Greek—the thing that has been made, the masterpiece, the poem. The Poiema Poetry Series presents the work of gifted poets who take Christian faith seriously, and demonstrate in whose image we have been made through their creativity and craftsmanship.

These poets are recent participants in the ancient tradition of David, Asaph, Isaiah, and John the Revelator. The thread can be followed through the centuries—through the diverse poetic visions of Dante, Bernard of Clairvaux, Donne, Herbert, Milton, Hopkins, Eliot, R. S. Thomas, and Denise Levertov—down to the poet whose work is in your hand. With the selection of this volume you are entering this enduring tradition, and as a reader contributing to it.

—D.S. Martin
Series Editor

COLLECTIONS IN THIS SERIES INCLUDE:

Six Sundays toward a Seventh by Sydney Lea
Epitaphs for the Journey by Paul Mariani
Within This Tree of Bones by Robert Siegel
Particular Scandals by Julie L. Moore
Gold by Barbara Crooker
A Word In My Mouth by Robert Cording
Say This Prayer into the Past by Paul Willis
Scape by Luci Shaw
Conspiracy of Light by D. S. Martin

What Cannot Be Fixed

JILL PELÁEZ BAUMGAERTNER

CASCADE *Books* • Eugene, Oregon

WHAT CANNOT BE FIXED

The Poiema Poetry Series

Copyright © 2014 Jill Peláez Baumgaertner. All rights reserved. Except for brief quotations in critical publications or reviews, no part of this book may be reproduced in any manner without prior written permission from the publisher. Write: Permissions, Wipf and Stock Publishers, 199 W. 8th Ave., Suite 3, Eugene, OR 97401.

Cascade Books
An Imprint of Wipf and Stock Publishers
199 W. 8th Ave., Suite 3
Eugene, OR 97401

www.wipfandstock.com

ISBN 13: 978-1-62564-586-9

Cataloging-in-Publication data:

Baumgaertner, Jill Peláez ; with a Foreword by Martin E. Marty.

    What Cannot Be Fixed / Jill Peláez Baumgaertner.

    The Poiema Poetry Series 12

    xii + 80 p. ; 23 cm.

    ISBN 13 : 978-1-62564-586-9

    1. American Poetry—21st century. I. Marty, Martin E. II. Title. III. Series.

PS3565.F247 2014

Manufactured in the USA.

To Martin, as ever

The word that came to Jeremiah from the Lord: "Come and go down to the potter's house, and there I will let you hear my words." So I went down to the potter's house, and there he was working at his wheel. The vessel he was making of clay was spoiled in the potter's hand, and he reworked it into another vessel, as seemed good to him.
—Jeremiah 18:1-3 (NRSV)

Let me hear joy and gladness; let the bones that you have crushed rejoice.
—Psalm 51:8 (NRSV)

Table of Contents

Foreword | ix
Acknowledgments | xi

I. Moving in the Unmade

The Creator Dreams Creation | 3
Ave and Benedicta | 5
Eve Speaks to Adam | 7
Prodigal Ghazal | 8
Conversion on Hearing *Pictures at an Exhibition* | 9
Ecclesiastes | 10
Grace | 11
Bilbao Alone | 12
Faith | 14
For a Birthday and Wedding Anniversary, Two Days Apart | 15
Frost Fires | 16
Easter Vigil | 18

II. The O Antiphons

Advent | 21
    The First Antiphon | 23
    The Second Antiphon | 24
    The Third Antiphon | 25
    The Fourth Antiphon | 26
    The Fifth Antiphon | 27
    The Sixth Antiphon | 28
    The Seventh Antiphon | 29

Table of Contents

III. Except for Woodworm

What Cannot Be Fixed | 33
For Sophie, Bald in Church | 35
What the Butcher Knows | 36
Persephone | 37
Bathsheba | 39
Let them | 41
Complex Phenomena | 42
Inertia | 44
My God, my God | 46

IV. Coming into Focus

Uprooted | 51
Cuba: 1979 | 52
Return Ticket | 54
Where Words Regain Their Meaning | 56
    I. Florida: 1951 | 56
    II. Buswell Library: 1995 | 56
    III. The Wade Center: 2001–2101 | 58
Story | 60
Leavings | 62
Spider | 64
Our Piano Teacher's Dock: A Sestina | 66
Un-titled | 68
Yorktown, Later | 71
My Father's Bones | 73
On the Road to Work | 74
The String Section Skinnydips | 75
Andrew Wyeth's *Distant Thunder* | 77
Deer Grass | 78

Foreword

Count them: you will find one exclamation point and twenty-six question marks in this collection of poetry. The exclamation point follows the command: "Listen!" in a shouted quotation she attributes to Pontius Pilate at the trial of Jesus. The other time the word "listen" appears, it is also part of a command, but now there is no exclamation mark, because it is the poet speaking, as if in a whisper. In a poem about an artist colony she pictures herself interrupting the silence with it during that "one second" before the baton of a conductor "bursts the music into bloom."

The question marks throughout the poems appear in more than a score of contexts, usually in utterances of the poet. Her general mode is invitatory. The reader is bidden to take part in her quests or to ponder her often ambiguous affirmations. Note that these *are* affirmations; they simply do not need to be thundered or delivered with thumps. Baumgaertner is not a confessional poet in the company of those who concentrate on themselves, whether their concentrations are revelatory or not. Yes, she can be autobiographical—in one poem the return of her father "again" from one of his three wars typically inspires curiosity about her life, but the self-references usually appear so that she can point to someone or something not enclosed and confined in the first person singular.

Those who are familiar with Jill Baumgaertner know that she lives a very full and, others would say, "busy" life as writer and editor of poetry, teacher and administrator of teachers, spouse and mother, citizen, and enjoyer of life. Yet the poems never suggest the stress characteristic of people who designate themselves as "busy." In musical terms, her work flows legato: there is nothing of the staccato of the sort we hear in so much poetry of our decades.

Foreword

As the lines of poetry flow, they bring us to many kinds of historical stops along the way. Baumgaertner is certainly at home with biblical narratives and concepts. We re-meet Eve and Bathsheba in poems which show the poet pondering womanhood. Theological concepts are here, but they are not burdened with technical apparatus for which one needs a philosophical lexicon. For example she slips in the little word 'sin' along with other profound signals about humans into narrative poems, where the reader is being handed a figurative mirror for self-examination. There is no hint of the didactic in these poems. We may learn much from them, but we are free to find meanings appropriate to our circumstances. They open the creative imagination to so many diverse experiences that one wonders why more contemporary poets do not frame their ponderings in theological terms.

When I mentioned "ambiguous affirmations" above, I had in mind examples such as those implied in "What Cannot Be Fixed," the title poem. The verb in that heading inspires curiosity. Baumgaertner and the violin repairman use "fix" as a synonym for "repair" as the first line of the poem suggests. You will not find that definition in historic dictionaries. Only in near-contemporary supplements to classical versions will lexicographers grant a few lines to "fix=repair," and then usually write off such usage to American, for example, as in "We Fix Flats.' Classically to "fix" has more to do with positioning, fastening, or attaching something securely. Reread line one of the poem: "Anything can be positioned securely." But ambiguity appears at once. The violin-maker and the poet list many things that are exceptions to his maxim, which means that they cannot be repaired.

We can attach that motif to Baumgaertner's affirmations. Yes, most everything can be secured, "except" where human frailty, divine hiddenness, and historical contingency come into play. This means that this poet cannot be written off as facile, glib, Polyannaish, just because she affirms. She says "yes" despite and in the face of the problematic, of evil, or tragedy. That is why those who accept the invitation to enter her world, insofar as poems can reveal it, are likely to reread her from time to time as their own circumstances change. The poetic lines, like the repaired ("fixed") violins, are handed to us, and "we handle them warily, uncertain how to touch these specimens of imperfection." But "touch them," we certainly shall, as, quietly and without a need for exclamation points, we are bidden to "listen."

Martin E. Marty

Acknowledgments

The author gratefully acknowledges the following publications in which many of the poems first appeared.

Ariel: "For Sophie, Bald in Church," "Persephone," "Florence's Dock: A Sestina"
The Christian Century: "Ave and Benedicta," "Bathsheba," "Story"
Christianity and Literature: "Spider"
The Cresset: "Conversion on Hearing *Pictures at an Exhibition*," "Easter Vigil," "What the Butcher Knows"
First Things: "Bilbao Alone," "Complex Phenomena"
Flourish: "The Creator Dreams Creation"
Fuel: "Cuba: 1979"
Image: "Prodigal Ghazal," "For a Birthday and Wedding Anniversary, Two Days Apart," "Deer Grass"
Notre Dame Review: "What Cannot Be Fixed," "The String Section Skinnydips"
Press: "Return Ticket"
Radix (www.radioxmagazine.com): "Inertia"
Roberts Writing Awards: "Yorktown, Later"
Second Opinion: "Un-titled"
Seven: "Where Words Regain Their Meaning"
Stauros Notebook: "Ecclesiastes," "Faith," "My Father's Bones"
Valparaiso Poetry Review: "Uprooted"
Vineyards: "My God, my God"

"Andrew Wyeth's Distant Thunder," Copyright © *Centennial Review* XXXX, no. 1 (Winter 1996): 92.
"Grace" first appeared in the Summer 2005 issue of Priscilla Papers (www.cbeinternational.org).
"Leavings" first appeared in the Spring 1995 issue of *River Oak Review.*

The Great O Antiphons: A Service for Advent. Poetry in meditations by Jill Baumgaertner, music by Carl Schalk. Minneapolis: Augsburg Fortress Press, 2013: "The First Antiphon," "The Second Antiphon," etc.
Leaving Eden. By Jill Peláez Baumgaertner. Fox River Grove, IL: White Eagle Coffee Store Press, 1995: "Eve Speaks to Adam," "Frost Fires."

Acknowledgments

My Father's Bones. By Jill Peláez Baumgaertner. Georgetown, Ky: Finishing Line Press, 2006: "Conversion on Hearing *Pictures at an Exhibition*," "My Father's Bones," "Ecclesiastes," "Grace," "Easter Vigil."

I also thank my assistant, Vera McDonald, who helped me prepare the manuscript.

I

Moving in the Unmade

*The maker moves
in the unmade, stirring the water until
it clouds, dark beneath the surface,
stirring and darkening the soul until pain
perceives new possibility. There is nothing
to do but learn and wait, return to work
on what remains. Seed will sprout in the scar.
Though death is in the healing, it will heal.*

—Wendell Berry

The Creator Dreams Creation

i.

The whole world, all of its grasses, oceans,
the tropical red blossoms opening to reveal
miniature villages of stamen and pistil.

The whole world knows its own beauty,
recognizes the gravity pull of poetry
into the crimson of itself, the peeling away
of oceans, the revelation of hibiscus,
the grasses' invitation to the horse.

Yet this is only the first stirring of the feather,
its most minute turning in a direction
before the motion begins. What follows,
what goes beyond this, is beauty.

ii.

The rivulet through the woods,
the water pooled on the shower floor,
the desert dew collected in pans,
the water of sunburn and dream,

All water flows to the sea
green with grief and tears,
green with hazard,
lower than all other waters,
creation's churn powerful with pull
and the humility of origins.

iii.

The dream silvers the day with longing.
The dream unravels back to origins.
The filament stretches from one blade tip of grass
to another, wafting in the slanted sunlight.

iv.

Light as sunlight
and warm, sunwarm,
this sand trickles from
between my fingers
as I uncurl fists of it,
not quite dust,
dreamwork for some
white winter morning.

v.

Like diving into the still lake
deep, deeper,
before the turning,
before the stretch
to break the grey surface.
This deep sleep, dreamless.

vi.

In dreams the road veers
off into deep water,
the pine-needled path
gives way to tangled brush,
and the still pond greens over.

The pattern is simple, clear,
its lines clean as right-angles.
Through the water I trail my hand.

Ave and Benedicta

Suddenly the rush of love,
thousands of wings flashing light,
the flood filling crevices and ditches with light.

The stone birds, the gargoyles' tongues lapping
the light as if it were milk; through glass
light pours like ribbons, grosgrain, silk,

needles of clear thread stitching, cross stitching,
impossibly embroidering diamonds on borders
as Eve stands in the mist of her own creation.

I am, she thinks, where I was not before. This is
as impossible as wondering how my words arrive
in my throat. Where do they curl before they uncurl?

And Adam, sandspurs adrift in his hair, has been
sleeping in the grass for a hundred years it seems
and, half-lidded, he thinks his dreams have made her up.

She points to sunlight and all he sees
are the straight lines from God floating motes
around and through. From his left-hand frame

where he had stood, one leg bent, he is moving slowly
through the flowers of Eden, oceans of grasses.
His former space is now a hollow of blackness,

background to itself. He is drawn to her flesh
so like his own, so much his own he wants to put it on.
But she is new in this knowledge and she has yet to know

how he is to do with her and why he now moves
across the canvas through the triptych garden
with its flourishes, its tiny flowers woven in the grass.

His thirst drives him forward, unbalancing the
altarpiece where now the center leans toward a second
Eve who stands within the enclosed garden

of her hinged panel looking beyond her book into
the sunlight, waiting for the angel's words to reach her.
She is rapt with love, she says yes to all creation,

knowing the image does not come
without the word.

She bears the Word.

Eve Speaks to Adam

The hydrangea creates its own colors,
its greens bursting blue and pink
sometimes at once on one silent stem,
emerging from a mute past into pastels,
background to each other.

Now you bend to cup the many-blossomed
blossom in two hands. How completely
it rests in your hold, trembling only
if you back away.

I remember the night-mist and you
on the ledge above the stone steps
having fled the garden that held close
my words to another creature, green
and golden in his promises.

Later I stared into my mirror until I
could not recognize the trembling as my
own. My image and the one reflected, unlinked.
Did I know you were my self, backing
away, unlacing fingers from fingers, moving
into the grey and silver of darkened mirrors?

You step now into the woven sunlight of the maple,
still green hinting at the yellow and orange,
the colored language of its letting go.
Which longing is mine? Which is yours?

Prodigal Ghazal

Weightless as a float into the drift of water, one whose sin is forgiven.
The Far Country a memory of fists and sour apples.

Of that old, heavy plunge through snowfall, frozen, refrozen.
The tug of gravity, slow and silent.

Of no words forming on dry lips, of breath aching to a full inhale and then a letting go.
Of not yet. Not yet. And the longing for release.

The hold of grimy pleasures like a small mouth forming very small o's.
Like spaces as vast as the tundra with no human voice or as tight as a wound spool.

The wasting disease of sin, God's serious hand of judgment.
Then His gentle push: the swing into the spring air, back and forth.

And then the breathing, unboxed. And later the fingers spread
Wide in the grass, each particular blade a tickle.

The Father runs into the road, his embrace a chunk of earth to the unmoored.
The twisted eyebeams, the Father's gaze into his son's tentative face.

Pupils black with light peering into the lens of revelation, crystalline.
Now comes the filling in of hunger, the bread hunks spilling crumbs.

The wine meant for throats dry with salt and dust.
Here is God, his strokes on our dead flesh

Filling capillaries, sparking nerves. We are fed with the crusts
And blood of forgiveness, with the thrill of its gentle float, its ripe music.

Conversion on Hearing *Pictures at an Exhibition*

After the light, mute as dust and flat,
after the colors' crisp disappearing entirely,
after the smother of warmed and rewarmed air,
the panic for breath,
after the thickening fatigue of arms, legs,
seeping to each finger's web
and each root of hair,
after all this and after the surgeon
carves your vessels like clay,
after he holds the heft of your heart
in his delicate fingers,
the needles' stitch his finest embroidery,

You awaken to sunlight
making its bright tracks through slit blinds,
and somewhere the bassoons and oboes
of Mussorgsky, the glockenspiel and flute,
the complexity of lines with the movement
of light, the sunlight both steady
and moving with shadows,

And you are certain God has flared out
like the sheen of lacquer on a silk-wrapped box,
like the sweep and arc of wing,
like the glisten on a wind-stirred pond.

Ecclesiastes

If, as the theologian says,
in creation God gives functions,
what, then, is the function of the dead
laid out in their tiny lots
like parked cars, their purpose
defined in their patch of green
or earth or stone, so orderly
next to willow or oak or highway,
glimpsed briefly through an open
window, reminding us of name
and time partitioned into life
and not, the interstice between
creation and absence spaced
by a hyphen?

Grace

Is it the transparency
and lift of air?
Is it release
as when the pebble
flings out of the slingshot
or the tethered dog
suddenly is without lead?

Or is it more like standing
on a dark beach
at midnight,
the surf loud
with its own revolution,
the horizon invisible,
the entire world the threat
of rushing water?

No one who swims
at night in the ocean
feels weightless
embracing armfuls of water
against the ballast
of the waves' fight.

Swimming:
toward the shore lights
or out into the vast bed
of the sea's white fires?

Bilbao Alone

Some of the sounds here are familiar:
Vivaldi plays the same in this language,
keys rattle in locks,

the engines of buses sigh as they turn street corners.
But something is different,
an odd solitude.

It digs itself under my watch into the small bones
of my wrist. Here in this place are no extras.
I play the leading role, but I am

as anonymous as my skeleton.
I have no drawers of envelopes and paper here,
no cupboards of glasses turned neatly upside down,

no simmering stews, no one whose knees fit
perfectly behind mine as I sleep.
Nothing of myself is here except myself.

What I have extends over vast landscapes
and it requires me to do nothing.
I sit in a park and watch what passes:

short Basque men whose tobacco lingers long after they
have gone, dogs whose interest is each other,
workmen with a ladder, the dignified bus

driver before the return trip, hands crossed behind.
And then suddenly it is twilight.
Sometimes one watches for no reason other than the eyes.

Is this grace, this waiting, a simple existing inside of it?
Is it always as ominous as these first few
hours of unfamiliarity?

Faith

It can be too careful,
a ledge-balancing
tiny slide of the foot
over slick surfaces.

When it finally happens,
                it should be more like a hurdle
                                into sudden air

off a cliff

faced with
    ragged signs
of the earth's upheaval,

or the rushed snatch of a demon
ferris wheel
that refuses to secure you
      with belt or rail
           and seizes you
up in its mechanical hands
to whisk
you
      higher,
            higher.

For a Birthday and Wedding Anniversary, Two Days Apart

Mornings their garden greens and flowers,
tomatoes ripen fat as babies' bellies,
hollyhocks tower straight-laced as fence rails.

This is not the black-topped yard of her childhood,
weedless, grassless, without tree bark or squirrel.

Here she follows behind her husband's wild planting.
Where Adam has sown, she is Eve weeding,
creating order in the simplicity of black earth,

clean around each plant's tuft or blossom,
important and particular. Like the tidy numbers
that track her check book or the organ she plays

with such precision, she sorts and arranges,
meticulous as her print on a fluted pie crust.

Tumbling back upon itself, this story with setting,
plot, and rising action begins with a scatter of water
on new flesh, pauses at the wedding altar for lovely entanglement,

leads always to the children, bright flesh prints,
and resolves around the moving point of a slender man,
her mate. Tomorrow they will rise

from their ordinary pew, front right, pulpit-side,
step carefully to the aisle, cup their hands for bread,
tip the chalice for wine, and join the narrative line

that stretches back before they were and reaches
forward, demanding blessing.

Frost Fires

In my neighbor's yard the mulberry which
has held beyond all reasonableness

is finally losing its
grip on stems dry with color.

The leaves have waited until there is no breeze.
The cold toast I leave for the birds balances

on the porch railing and I hear the *tip-tit* of leaf
falling on frozen leaf, the background to birdsong,

so natural seeming I am hardly aware
that now at this precise instant the leaves

are letting go. The tree has wrestled itself away
from night, has sketched itself against first light

and now finally flicks its leaves off one by one,
stiffening into its winter pose.

The spears of sunlight that glance off roof shingles
sparkling with morning frost

catch me and I see that I, too, am drawn in front
of a backdrop effusive with blue.

Is this a sign, the way the last fall falls? I know
only that last night's rain, now stiff puddles,

iced the leaves from the season's leaf fall—and still
the mulberry clung. Thousands have crumbled,

no, hundreds of thousands of crisp brown leaves,
red, softer yellows, the fires of the season

compressed and formal now that small piles
of them are frozen under the glaze of rain.

But only now these particular leaves fall at perfect
intervals that count the seconds and half seconds off

like a competition in a game of tensile strength.
It's mainly branches now and at the base of the trunk,

one geranium, still fiercely hanging on to red.

Easter Vigil

From the church's side door we follow the candle
held aloft in the uncertain spring evening, this dead time
between death and birth, treading the pavement to the opened
narthex door, the procession silent as dusk. Our tapers flare
briefly as they steal flame, then settle into small, steady burns,
each a puncture to the gathered darkness of the sanctuary.

The human story – the rebellions, the redemptions – read
in darkness, the light to some a present shimmer, to most
a dim promise. And you, two brothers, sitting in the deepened
shadows, not quite sure that this hushed service is really
yours, knowing only that your time has almost come.
When the congregation gathers at the font, you stand

shifting your weight, ready now for drowning,
your palms moist. How can this birth be so like death,
you wonder, its public nature almost humiliation?

What happens next is water and movement, then into the fulgent
chancel fragrant with bright narcissus, lily, bread and wine,
the celebration of rising. I recall this now as we awaken
each morning to the stunned wonder of how you could be
one moment and not the next, the child whose forehead once
glistened with sprinkled water, now sunk in the baptism of death.

You know what we do not—the lifting up out of it, the first
gasps of birth, but we linger behind you, words smothered,
motion stopped, lips dry with what we hardly dare believe.

What comes after this vacancy, after the stripped altar
and God's Friday silence? We do not want the cross
the season thrusts upon us. But once again it is our turn.

Our hands cupped, the host pressed into it, the quickening
of the wine, the animating of all from nothing, nuclei, protoplasm –
jellylike, colloidal – the chromosomes, genes, DNA, infused
with movement, tempo, the beating of the heart, the pinking
of the skin, the soft breathing of the sleeper breaking
into wakefulness, eyes opening to effortless light.

II

The O Antiphons

ADVENT

The First Antiphon

O Wisdom, proceeding from the mouth of the Most High, pervading and permeating all creation, mightily ordering all things: come and teach us the way of prudence.

Prudence is not a word
we love. It inhibits our choice.
We prefer the allure of tinsel
and artifice, the relentless
tug toward the flesh
of a paltry beauty.

And we inhabit a planet
of uncertainty.
Who is the friend
and where the enemy,
as we are pulled
this way and that?
We extend our hand
or should we fight
instead?

Now Wisdom speaks,
parsing, separating,
reordering, steering us
from quicksand's brink,
the enfleshed Word
steady on firm terrain.
We balance there
between yes and no.

We await him.
Come, Lord Jesus.

The Second Antiphon

> *O Adonai and ruler of the house of Israel, who appeared to Moses in the burning bush and gave him the Law on Sinai: come with an outstretched arm and redeem us.*

The Law sculpts our sin
in *bas relief*. We trace
its outline, rehearse
its shape, feel once again
its heft.

We cannot rest easy
watching Moses face
the heat of the bush,
removing his shoes
on hallowed ground.

Our shoes remain.
We are rooted here
but desperate to weave
in and out for old
advantages.

We crave release,
the spring of warmed
muscles, Adonai's
arm outstretched.
Redemption.

We await him.
Come, Lord Jesus.

The Third Antiphon

O Root of Jesse, standing as an ensign before the peoples, before whom all kings are mute, to whom the nations will do homage: come quickly to deliver us.

Here in the dust
we are astonished
by the root's tenacity,
the only life in a ruined
and dead land.
It stirs underground,
pushes through rock,
ferns curled,
leaves folded,
buds tightly wound,
the bloom finally
loosening and opening
in a place of broken
images and dry breath.

We await him.
Come, Lord Jesus.

The Fourth Antiphon

O key of David and scepter of the house of Israel, you open and no one can close, you close and no one can open: come and rescue the prisoners who are in darkness and the shadow of death.

Shackled in the obscurity
of our prison, locked in,
solipsistic, we see only
our own sin,
unable to escape
our insufficiencies.

But the promise of release
has been there all along.
We pluck the key
from our bosom
and the chains release,
the prison door opens.
There in our baptism
is our freedom.
All we have ever needed
to do is remember it.

We await him.
Come, Lord Jesus.

The Fifth Antiphon

*O dayspring, splendor of light everlasting: come and enlighten
those who sit in darkness and in the shadow of death.*

In December already at four o'clock
in the afternoon, shadows overtake us
and only the treetops catch the last
slant of sunlight. Then the darkness
deepens beyond all imagining,
this darkness of spirit which admits
no glimmer or ray.

Here in the sanctuary the Advent candles,
lit one by one, week by week,
first pinpricks then lengthening flame,
gather the light and focus it.

The days begin to lengthen imperceptibly
and now, finally, is the time for new light—
the faint dawn, the first, tiny signs.
Now is the time for a paling sky,
pink at the tree line.

We await him.
Come, Lord Jesus.

The Sixth Antiphon

O king of the nations, the ruler they long for, the cornerstone uniting all people: come and save us all, whom you formed out of clay.

The Word that shaped creation
spun the dust, gathered the seas,
carved the clay, sparked the life.

This Word more than the un-Worded
words of careless speech. This Word
the gospel, the cornerstone, the king
who shatters the darkness,
who gives sight, who becomes the bright
fleshprint of incarnation.

This is the remote become immediate,
the abstract made concrete, the dream
become certain. This is the birth-marked
Word that created our senses
and opened them. He breathes
on us and we live.

We await him.
Come, Lord Jesus.

The Seventh Antiphon

O Emmanuel, our king and our lawgiver, the anointed of the nations and their Savior: come and save us, O Lord our God.

Emmanuel, God with us,
knows what our flesh knows:
the itchiness of wool against skin,
the lingering taste of wine,
the glossiness of leaves after rain,
the press of earth clods underfoot,
the grit of sawdust on hands.

This is the mystery:
King and carpenter's son,
Shepherd and Lamb,
God of Jacob and son of David.
With outstretched arms
he redeems us, the purple
of royalty and passion
emblazoning
the world's darkness.

We await him.
Come, Lord Jesus.

III

Except for Woodworm

> *I need not have stood long*
> *Mocked by the smell of a mown lawn, and yet*
> *I did. Sickness for Eden was so strong.*

—Elizabeth Jennings

What Cannot Be Fixed

Anything can be repaired,
the violin-maker says,
except for woodworm
or the violin inside
the fire-melted case.

A violin is more than its own strings'
sound, the wood thin and flexible,
loose for sympathetic resonance,
leaning into the cello's timbre,
leaning into your own voice.

Things can go wrong, he says.
The glue must not petrify
the instrument. Even the soundpost
sometimes eats the wood and begins
to push its way through.

Or the fingerboard can loosen
and warp the soundboard.
Or a person changing bad strings
can release tension
so fast the soundpost shifts.

Or the instrument can be fraudulent,
aged with artificial nicks,
fake repairs. But most can be fixed
again, he says, the last button
missing on his shirt.

Repairing a violin is like stitching
something which is torn,
he says, rocking on his heels,
unwrapping necks, wood,
damaged violins to pass among us.

We handle them warily, uncertain
how to touch these specimens
of imperfection, blackened by fire,
crushed by the car's fender,
caught in the flooded basement,
frozen in the abandoned car.

For Sophie, Bald in Church

The others on whom cancer
also closes in wear wigs or scarves
but your head is bare

and smooth as a peach.
You wear it cleanly
and there is no Auschwitz

agony in your eyes although
you also know that other type of
baldness sour and silent. But now you

ask about what happens later—
if the soul hovers in the out there
floating in dreams waiting

for the body to catch up.
And we in our habitual pews
sit behind you and see the cross

through the penumbra of your
head—naked as an infant
still curling into its mother.

What the Butcher Knows

How to dismember,
how to separate the fat,
how the muscles stick to the bone
how to detach wings
how to loosen joints
how to smack pink coils into a paper boat.

Every morning he puts on
a freshly starched apron
and unsheathes his knife from the carving block;
he walks through the freezer jostling
sides of beef, setting them moving like
impatient children standing on one
foot and then the other.

He knows about the insides of things,
tucking the neck into the hollow chicken,
stuffing sausages into translucent socks.

Probably also he knows
what to do with feathers,
brains, hooves.

Wrapping packages of prim chops,
he sees beyond today.
He knows how things turn out if they
are not snatched up.

Persephone

On earth the light crept even
in the middle of her sleep inside
her lids to form the moving shapes
that drifted into mandalas of dreams.

In hell she had no dreams. There was not room enough
in darkness for her images. Her depthlessness
of sleep was black and she felt no
sharp boundaries between awake and dead.

And claustrophobia—
the spiders that could live without the sun
spun webs without dimension, with lines that moved
upon themselves, but never out.

Space was as far as she could reach
or torch could light.
It was the smallest feeling in the universe.
She was a mere interstice, a gentle heap

of flesh between two worlds.
When Hermes went to hell to find Persephone,
he hardly knew whose face he gazed upon,
she had so changed. Her gestures now

were malleable, unfixed. Profusion
crowded, turned upon itself.
Her favorite words were no and not.
She thought of nothing more and more.

When Hermes took her by the hand, she thought
escape and end, release, but not return.
Her husband forced the pomegranate seed
between her lips. Involuntarily, she bit

and his smile now was definite and swift.
He knew the magic of the seed had made
hell's tug cyclic necessity.
Persephone now walks eight months on earth

and spends the other four with him.
With him her life is necrological.
With him nonbeing's lure negates her energies,
puts her to sleep.

Without him she creates the season's turn,
she grows the twigs too green for snapping
and deepens grass, but now
her dreams are tinged with shadows

and her early morning images—
the leaves—which dry
and crisp themselves
toward fall.

Bathsheba

She was completely clean, her skin
smelled of water and silk,
her hair tendrilled in its damp.
His messenger had rushed her dressing,

but she had pulled on an
arm of bracelets that rattled
when she lifted the hand David now
pulled to his mouth. And then with his

embrace she fit, just so, and shed
her bracelets one by one.
The echoes of their rolling clanks
unstilled the water in the nearby pool.

When she went home she rearranged Uriah's
store of wine, she handled swords he'd trained
with from his youth. She wanted patterns,
plans, arrangements, certainties.

David remembered how the light seemed
more like the drift of afternoon as he
leaned against the window and watched
those below crossing the road at four

corners, mid-morning. He was the boy
somewhat and somewhat not—whitened hair,
a few new lines—his eyes on her, the whiteness
of her flesh so much his earth,

so much his desire. He could have known
the wrench of loss ahead, the child unfolded
from its mother's womb stretched into death
within a week. But he chose not to.

One death so much like any other, he thought—
maneuvered or dreaded, they are all, finally,
sacrifices. Did he believe her nod meant
acquiescence? It meant she saw the truth

but could not speak it in syllables that he would
hear. It meant she would not pour her protest
into the stream of his desire that stretched across
landscapes straight as a wall. It meant he would think

reserve when she meant no. So she acceded
to wordlessness, her only power to spread her
silences before him, as carefully patterned as a
score of music, as reflective as polished stones.

Let them

Matthew 19

He names them: Samuel, Isaac, Mary,
all of the anonymous daughters of Jephthah,
the infant of Bathsheba,
and those forty-two children who laughed
at bald Elisha and were torn limb from limb.

Let them come.
Let them push their small shoulders
into the crowd of Rachel's children.
Let the Holy Innocents stand so close
they can see the beating pulse
of his temple.

Let them come.
All those with delicate wrists,
small ankles, pudgy or thin arms,
round bellies from feast or famine.
Let them feel the breath of God
On their precarious necks.

Let the armless child from Iraq
rest on his knee. Let the Vietnamese
girl with burning skin remember
his cool fingers.

Let them come. Do not hinder them.
Smooth the path, clear the way
for him to feel the press of them,
the warmth of their perilous bodies
next to his.

Complex Phenomena

The rules of chaos are simple: A mountain
is never a perfect cone. A lake
is never really a circle. A drop

of dew is not a microcosm.
No. Flowers wither.
Dust collects. There is

the relentless return of what we
do not want. Everything inclines
to disorder. But then how

to explain this grove of orange trees
planted so close branch nuzzles branch,
the whole world in permanent rows?

An illusion, of course. When
the present for most of us lasts only
3 seconds. But then how to

explain the man blind from birth who
sees a person and believes he sees
a tree on legs? How did he find

the conceit to link such disparates?
The tactile vision of his past creates the
chaos of his present sightedness.

His world, newly angled, is no longer
reasonable, but still he relies on what
he knows. He names what he sees, revising

phylum, genus, class as he goes,
sometimes standing quite still, eyes closed
in order to recall the harmony of things.

Inertia

I

Somewhere someone is hammering,
a caged dove coos,
her flight rattle silenced. Pilate

stands, one hand on his hip,
his palms sticky, fresh from
morning plums, so ripe

the juice as it trickled down his throat,
as he bit into flesh
as dark as his mouth.

II

*Are you the King of the
Jews?* he asks,
and before the last word leaves

Pilate's mouth, the other
one says, *You say so,
Jew* and *You*

blending into the answer
latent in the seamless
interrogative.

III

The others yell their threats,
their old fears, their questions
of both. They are a garble of anger.

Then Pilate once again:
*Listen! Do you not hear their
complaints?* Jesus is not resigned.

This is the quiet of termites.
It is the silence of the vein of silver
underneath the mountain's

grimace, helpless to resist the mud's
cracked reclumping, the boulders'
stance nudged into acceleration,

the ground once steady and dependable
now curling under the earth's crust
rumbling under its elastic waves.

My God, My God

His ragged cry, threads trailing,
a cry full of nails, rips, tears, tēars,
the cry spilling over the full cup
he has taken. Not like a fountain,

bubbling over, but like a mound
of sand, piled high, giving way,
falling grain on grain burying
the burrowing crab almost impossibly

as he does his dark work.
The cry of God to God, desperate,
the question whose answer
is the silence—of the dirt scattered

on the lowered coffin, of the lull
of sea between waves, of the depth
of roots stretched in dark earth
beneath grass, cracking cement,

twisting under pavement, threading
into culverts. *Every night
has something of Gethsemane,*
the theologian says, a shattered

day left behind, then deep night
and sleep and only much later
the awakening to breath
and new light. But for now this

is the present through which
the future becomes the past.
We cling to his cry, our God,
who now knows what we know—

a mute paralysis. No words.
No response. God lives his silence,
our God who now feels his grief,
his questions, his absence.

IV

Coming into Focus

Don't tell me the moon is shining;
show me the glint of light on broken glass.

−Anton Chekhov

Uprooted

The artists painting Cuba from memory
or from photographs, from family stories
of the Exodus, from dreams, know
their bloodlines are not clear. The work
is mongrel, neither Cuban nor American.

They paint masks, figures floating, palm
trees set on pedestals. They sculpt women
locked in birth. What they want is a particular
place. What they find is borrowed space.
In hand-colored gelatin silver prints or wood

with oil and gold leaf or oil on linen or on
masonite or on carved locust bark, they discover
new rooms, dream landscapes, regions of origin
as small as phone-booths, as expansive as cane
fields, rented, tenanted, temporary.

Interprete mi silencio, one says.
They are like poets scratching out their
metaphors sideways on pieces of lined paper,
crossgrain, drafting possibilities,
unsettled, undecided.

These artists ask and never receive replies,
remember without mementos, feel without touching.
They have heard of the royal palm, seventy feet tall
and seek its landscape. How odd its trunk
is almost hollow, its roots mere threads.

Cuba: 1979

No indoor plumbing, the *excusado* is behind
the thatched hut built of rough planks, unpainted,
the front of the *bohío* painted bright blue,
the narrow paths lined with white
periwinkles to be cut and boiled for eyewash.

"*¿Porqúe?*" Elena asks. "Why is it that shame
always falls on the one who shows the belly,
not on the one who caused it?"

The zinc bathhouse roof next to the *bohío*,
the water falling inside in a fine spray
from the sprinkler, the metal tank above,
heated by the sun. The soap on the windowsill,
the small hole in the cement floor for drainage
through a pipe that disappears into the ground.
A piece of cheesecloth for a door. Elena says,
"Sometimes less is better."

In Elena's house the Virgin's statue in the bedroom,
Fidel's picture on the living room wall.

"*Compañera*," she says. "What does Fidel
have to do with the Virgin? He's not *una
fantasía*. The Virgin was my grandmother's
whose lifelong prayers were answered by Fidel.
No praying to dolls for my children.
Still, I can't throw her away.

"I don't deny it. I pray sometimes. Not that
I believe, *no creo*, it's just that I don't stop
believing either. Besides, it's better to pray just
in case. It doesn't hurt. I work hard. I am
'*una madre en acción*.' Everyone knows
me. I never fail the *Revolución*.

"But, *mala suerte*, I have had a time with
my daughter. She is fourteen. The local boy
returned from *los militares* and took her home.
He sent her back when she was boring him.
A man *sufre nunca* when he runs around. A woman—
it takes only one man for *desgracia*."

Elena picks up the broom to sweep the house again.
Like a nun at prayer she does it eight times a day.
This is vespers.

Return Ticket

The ladies on the Miami-Havana flight
remember the white dresses of their mothers,
their tiny feet and perfect nails.
They remember the clear colors of Cuba:
the yellow, green and blue facades.
They remember the verandas, the clubhouse
and the Hotel Nacional. They remember
the iron-barred windows, the bullet-proof doors,
the mosquito netting as profusely draped
as the Virgin's gown, fold upon fold,
tucked, billowing, liberally arranged.

They remember closets filled with silken frocks
and calfskin shoes, ball gowns, wedding dresses.
They remember officials keen to uncover flight,
to discover too much luggage, too many jewels,
signs that only half of a roundtrip ticket
ever would be used. One lady remembers her mother
wrenching off her diamond and giving it
to the officer inspecting the bags. "Here," she said,
"I will leave this with you for safekeeping."

The expulsion from their island was not forced.
They could have stayed. They could have watched
their villas of white marble and jasper
transformed into maternity homes and schools.
They chose to pack necessities, to smuggle money,
to leave for Miami, Boston, Jacksonville, New York.

They return to Cuba now to visit Isabel, Marisa,
Elena, Dioni, Maria, those who stayed because their husbands
would not leave, because their mothers were ill,
those with tiles missing from the kitchen walls,
those who every morning pour a second round of hot water
through the damp coffee grounds.

One woman remembers the family's haste,
each of her uncles thinking the other had arranged
their eldest sister's passage, leaving
her by mistake alone in the mansion, her Louis XV chairs
growing dingy with dust and moths, the carpets,
silver, furniture sold one by one to keep her in okra and rice.

The ladies on the Miami-Havana flight wear gaudy
hats and they are fat with clothes: two blouses,
vests, stockings stuffed into pockets, bottoms
huge with a bustle of rolled up jeans, packages
of coffee, rice, flour, bras filled with chorizos.
They have pinned lace, ribbons, earrings, bracelets
to their hats. The airline limits luggage, but they
cannot limit a person's weight. They attach
the WalMart goods and fill themselves
with merchandise: colanders, radios, pressure cookers.

The ladies on the Havana-Miami flight return hatless.
They have waists and small breasts.
They are imprinted with the kisses of sisters,
brothers, cousins, bruised by the farewell embraces.
Only now as they doze briefly before Miami do they allow
themselves to drift back to when all the bells in Havana
rang at daylight—every church, every square, every tower,
raucous with daylight, the dozen cane-bottom rocking chairs
arranged in two even lines in each sitting room, stirred
slightly into motion, the dozen cuspidors glinting with sunrise.

Where Words Regain Their Meaning

       I.

    Florida: 1951

The child you once were
sits on the porch swing in the heat
weighted with summer rain.
Grandmother points to each word.
You repeat, "Good morning, Baby.
Good morning, Baby Ray."
And the longing is unlatched,
the hunger for words that transcend
the world locked into the safety
of Mother's lunches,
of Father's Saturday mornings,
of Grandmother's books stacked
beneath her bed or behind glass doors.

Behind the barriers of ciphers
marching across a page the mysteries
are revealed with your first mouthing
of consonants crisped by unfamiliarity
and vowels forcing the syllables
into language which becomes more than speech.
This is your first transcendence.

      II.

    Buswell Library: 1995

The pleasant mustiness of old books,
the stiffened bindings of the new
and the smell of ink, paper, glue,

and you have found your way again.
The college stacks, the secluded
carrels, the whisper-squeak
of the librarian's cart.

Up the back stairs into the room
called Kilby, quiet with the hush
of study, the scratch of pen,
a muffled rattle of ideas.

This is the place where words regain
their meaning, the books—Tolkien,
Chesterton—packed in like bricks—
Sayers, Lewis, MacDonald—
and parked on tabletops—Barfield,
Williams. Occasionally, a spray
of dust-moted sun
and through the windows a glimpse
of the unwritten world outside these words.

You have missed entire seasons
inside such spaces (the ripening of summer,
the blazing of fall), besotted with words,
breaking print into patterns,
tracing images, wrestling language
amidst the indiscipline of marginalia
in rooms like this filled with the whisperings
of words, not words that fall back inside
themselves like ice on a thawing pond,
but words that disperse to fill a space,
like breath that weaves the pliant silence
into the warp and woof of music.

III.

The Wade Center: 2001–2101

After the months of cement-pouring,
the raising of walls, the bracing
of floors with book-supporting trusses.
After the roofers carefully treading
the sloped surfaces. After the sawdust,
the construction trailers parked behind Edman
in the snow, the temporary front door,
the chimney pots on order, the blueprints
spread on saw-horsed plywood,
the staircases without railings.
After the packing and unpacking of files,
the book boxes stacked six feet high,
the paths between them like a garden maze,
we wander new spaces, pristine,
not yet redolent of concentrated reading,
not yet filled with the rustled silence
of scholars, the children's corner a mere outline,
Aslan's portrait leaning against a wall,
Lewis's bust stashed in a safe corner.

You who follow, you yet unborn,
you will know these spaces for the first time,
too. You will grow familiar, as will we,
with the patterns formed by sunlight
through this glass, with the heft
of the door, with books now older,
their pages brittled by the years.

Think back on us, the new millennium
handed to us like an unproofed book.
You will supply it with words as yet unfleshed,
correcting what we discerned
as mere glimmers and flashes.

Yet you, too, will have your blindnesses.
That "chaos of stark bewilderment" Sayers
saw one Ash Wednesday in the middle
of a century of bones, you will know, too.

Direct your gaze to the garden,
which to us is no more than the promise soil holds.
There in the nodding daffodils of early spring,
the sweet pea, the day lily, the delphinium
of summer, the phlox and cleome,
the sudden arbor, the rose, the boxwood hedge
precisely trimmed, there you will find
a partial answer to disorder,
the rupture in the stem opening to blossom.

Turn back now to the books before you.
Find there in the uncharted
middle of your life the deep woods
of the Word. You must not hesitate.
Step inside.

Story

The silences of his brothers when Peter
married Agnes pushed them finally
down the Georgia hills to Florida
where Peter now sits in the webbed chair

on his front porch built
around a tree reaching through the roof.
Every day Agnes waters it with the melted ice cubes
from the glasses she finds about the house.

Peter watches everything: cars passing, the flutter
of a leaf, and across the road a woman in short
yellow culottes and a duckbill hat walking
down the fairway followed

by her caddy. The pressure is again
in Peter's chest. He cannot swallow.
In her white dress that she saves for errands
Agnes is coming up the walk.

He must tell her—
before she has time to wipe the perspiration
from her upper lip or drop her packages on
the porch swing. About the time

the glass door was thrown back,
the late spring finally pressing through the haze
of the screen and connecting its new-gold
with the *coo-ah, coo coo* of the doves

the same as always but new, as spring always is.
He must tell her what he saw once at the river,
his mother on the shore dipping her hands into
the water, rubbing her face. His brother in the white

robe wading to his knees to meet the preacher
in the middle of the water.
But here now is the unction
of her white dress against a sky blue with pain.

Leavings

Korea was my father's second war of three
and as I tugged at the sheets with my mother
each morning, helping her roll the pillows
and tuck the spread in, the radio would intone
the names of casualties. I was to listen for his
name but not to hear what I was listening
for, my mother said. This is my memory.

I know now that is not the way it happens.
A government car stops beside the house.
One knows, as soon as the dog barks
the warning, what is coming next.

But what I remember is pressing my fingernail
into the soft wood of the pale dresser, the crescent
that appeared so perfect that again I indented
wood and again, first with one thumbnail, then
the other, forming parentheses within parentheses.
When I finished, I positioned the dresser scarf
to cover the scarred wood, thinking my mother
might never find it although I knew she often
looked for what she didn't want to find—dirt,
mosquitoes, lice, chicken pox. When she found
the blemishes, I shook my head, but she fit
my fingers to the marks like Cinderella's slipper.

What my mother did that day in 1952 when I
was four and had filled the wood with punctuation
was lift my heavy hair, brush it and cut it to my ears,
the blade's keenness snipping, finding more than I
knew was there, as I watched my hair disappear and
a new face emerge like a picture coming into focus
through a lens—cheeks, eyes, chin.

I remember my father's return, maybe then,
maybe from another TDY, opening his suitcase
on the living room floor in the middle of the night,
pulling out a sleek brown fur for mother, blue
and pink satin jackets with embroidered dragons,
and a Japanese doll, porcelain skin as smooth
as the smoothest egg shells, thick hair that smelled
of glue, bluntly cut hair as black and shiny
as the radio beside my parents' bed.

When I awoke, I thought I'd dreamed it until I saw
her on the ebony stand, the gold threads in her red
kimono catching sunlight, and morning in its own space
again. My father, as naturally as breathing, lay in my
mother's bed before he left again and again.

Spider

The spider is there under the edge
of the carpet, in the corner
of the shower stall, on the drapery cord
or hiding behind the books

in the glass case
and I know it will suddenly
be there on my hands,
in my hair, scattering

its stringy legs on the inside
of my collar. Great-grandad without legs
lies in his bed,
lies there with his grin

and his arms reach to the swing
bar and he lifts himself out of bed
and into the wheelchair
where he lights his pipe

and breathes huge rattling coughs
and sits next to the oil heater
we dress around in the winter.
Undershirts, white cotton pants,

crinolines, pressed dresses, buttoned
sweaters. My sister puts on her winged
glasses that overwhelm her small face
and her legs are so skinny

in her underwear. She pushes her nose
up to make it more pug she says
and looks pointedly at mine. I grab
my thighs from underneath and pull

the flesh tight and nothing moves when I
bounce my foot. That is what it should be,
I think, just a little flesh and the rest bone.
The spider has begun its trek along the long

desert of the carpet and my sister picks it
up by one leg and pulls it off. She flicks
it in the air and it disappears,
as light as dust.

Our Piano Teacher's Dock: A Sestina

The dock, weathered grey and splintered, pricking the insides
of our knees when we'd sit swinging our legs, skimming
lightly the water's surface, scratching
it with our toes. We'd hop off the dock
into the water and squish out into the lake,
the clear water, the mud exploding around our toes,

the tiny fish flinging themselves beyond our toes
beyond the rippled water that lapped against the inside
of our legs. This was Florence's lake
and her squat house, the grasses skimming
the double-tracked road that led to the dock,
and inside, the piano covered with fringed shawls, the scratching

of dragonflies as they hit the screen, the cat scratching
her ear. The polish on Florence's toes
bright pink as she slapped back from the dock
in her flip flops, as she tracked sand inside
her house onto her thin rugs filled with grit skimmed
from the weeds and sand that clung to feet still damp from the lake.

We'd dig our fists into the lake
until we felt the scratch
of something new and skim
the dripping mud off mussel shells, mud sucking our toes
so deep they seemed inside
the bottom of the lake far from the dock.

At dusk we'd stretch out on the dock
and watch the turtles break the surface of the lake
so still then, her piano playing drifting to us from inside
her heavy parlor. We felt clean, the air smooth, we scratched
our old mosquito bites, we flexed our toes
and watched the fishes skim

the water's bug-crusted skin. Her ringed fingers skimmed
the keys as we snagged splinters in the knotty planks of her old dock.
The piano pedals' clunking rhythm curled her toes
around them and the music of the nighttime lake
would lap her girlish ribbons in her lake-grey hair, and scratch
her lapsed and softened flesh, her rooms inside.

With Florence we skimmed time inside
her dark piano's dampened tones, outside the docks scratched
stretch of rotting wood. Our whitened toes are tender from the
wrinkles of her lake.

Un-titled

Each time the parking garage light
blinks FULL and we begin
down one-way streets
turning at odd intervals
until finally—there—
the vacancy that barely fits.
We enter the building

with locked stairwells, exiting
the elevator at the murals
of water, trees, and paths
leading away somewhere.
My daughter who sits beside me
has felt the stirring of charms inside
her head and she shakes them away.

She shakes her head again.
She has had weeks of brain-work.
Pictures. Flashing lights. Charts.
Vials of her blood neatly labeled,
minutely examined.
But now her clean hair falls to its side part
as she bends over a magazine and when

the man appears, smiling, she follows
him without looking back at me.
Inside her head are images—
both flowers and rats—
circulating with molecules of oxygen
branching with nerves
reaching her polished fingertips, even her lips,

where sometimes she strikes them loose
into the words these people ask for.

But there is a problem.
There can be no real words here
in this corridor of closed doors.
She sits now behind one of them.
A person asks her questions and she replies.

I can feel the undertow of their voices
although the words are blurred
and always sink away from me. I ride
on their cadences and am pulled finally
toward an ever-receding hostility.
Perhaps this is a genetic tendency,
an imbalance of brain chemistry.

The words used here have glassy surfaces.
I can hear the abysses underneath their enamelled shells.
The door opens, the man smiles and shakes my hand.
(Every image, I tell my students, should do
two things at once.)
Nothing is lost on him. My hands are sweaty.
He has taken this idea and made it into a system.

My daughter fits a certain category, he says,
as all the others have.
The traffic outside occasionally intrudes,
a horn, a bus stopping and then starting again.
We once again get back into ourselves,
pretend this is a normal summer afternoon,
and we have come to the city to shop.

Pretend I will go home to the kitchen
where the bread that has spent
all afternoon rising now will
golden and firm.
She will make iced tea
and sit on the counter,
swinging her bare feet against the cabinet

door below. She will watch the squirrel
scratch on the window screen as he does
every evening. Pretend now that she
unlatches the screen, hands him a small warm crust.
Pretend now that this time on hind legs
he reaches for it with his teeth,
his tiny hand brushing her sleek thumbnail.

Yorktown, Later

Three chandeliers grey with sea mornings
hang in the entrance of the Seafood Pavilion.
Across the street is the river and the P.O.,
maybe the only one in Virginia with its own sea wall.

She has brought a green webbed chair, but she
does not sit in it. She cleans the fish and attaches the
offal with twist ties to the inside of the crab cage.
She is pregnant and her ankles, swollen

with toxemia, are invisible. Her leg meets her foot
in a grim line. Her cooler is full of crabs
shuffling slowly over ice. She casts the cage
and pulls it in again as her child, blonde,

knees darkened with dirt and tan, says, "Mommy,
let me this time. Let me,
Mommy." She does not nod or shake her head.
She does not lift her voice. She murmurs nothing.

She casts the cage again.
My husband stands here with me. He yearns
for an inlet or a creek off this river.
He would like to steer his motor boat at five a.m.

into a damp dawn noisy with gulls. Four months
after his father's death, this place like a pulley
carries him with no drag at all to the Jones Mill Pond
and the Naval Weapons Pier he fished as a crew-cut kid,

his dad baiting the hooks with worms and bread.
We have spent the afternoon driving the bricked
roads of the county. We have stopped at Yorktown
battlefield and read the historical markers. We have

walked the river paths. We have found Nick's Seafood Pavilion
where he had been brought with his birthday watch huge
on his wrist, his dad passing the bread basket and telling
him to order fish now, this is the bay, and when

the flounder arrived it was as large as a frying pan.
The world presents itself in twos: he and his father
on one side of the table, his mother and sister on the other.
A fifth does not fit into this picture, the fourth cannot

be taken away, no matter how he cuts and pastes the pieces.
I stand apart from his grief, as far away as the mother and
child on the wharf, as far away as her crabs are from
ever seeing the river bottom again. He has encased this death.

He has stretched layer upon layer carefully, tightly
fastening the leaves around the core, hard as a cabbage.
From her lead the woman walks the crab cage
through the water one last time and pulls it in. Her child

sucks a purple popsicle and stares at the thin lines
of wake a passing boat has pushed aside. My husband
lifts his camera, and puts my sideways glance
into the picture, another photo of one of us alone

in the center of a world we briefly knew. Later he will say
that he returned to a place and it was the same
and not the same. Later I will say that the water took
on the gold of the sun in a thin path away from us.

My Father's Bones

The pale green smoke of trees in early spring,
your ashes in a box in Mother's closet.
The whorl of your fingerprints, given up, dust
sealed in a carton, your bones a shiver
of powder, your breath mere evaporation.

In dreams you are now a silent driver through countries
of my childhood, your elbow on the open window,
your tonsured head a fringe of hair.
You steer the way between worlds,
I a passenger, the hot wind in my face.

Why are you here? I want to ask. I can ask
anything. I prompt myself, *Ask.*
But the questions curl up in my throat and you
Are where you belong, unfrazzled, calm,
a bit distant, your mind now on things that matter.

Like a wasp hovering against a screen door,
wanting in, wanting in, I live the presence
of your absence, unable to push through this hazy
barrier to where you are. Like a hand pushing
a rounded palm of wind from the passenger's window.

Like gravity, these connections to your crumbled
flesh, invisible, substantial. Once again the return
of April, but your path is linear, not these fat thumbs
of green thrusting through the soil damp with winter's
last snow, not the straightening spines of ferns unfurled,

but a tapestry unraveling its weave, unthreading back
to mats and yarn, to hemp and wool, to origins.

On the Road to Work

On the road to work
tree pollen whirls like ash
caught in the draft of passing cars
scattering powder
while branches are still laden
with tightly furled leaves
and buds waiting for their entrance
into a full season.

I dreamed last night of my mother
at some odd resort of swamp
and lush grasses all the way
to the open water.

She waited to board the boat.
I ran back to the room
for some forgotten thing
and then could not get back
to her, the water rising,
the separation absolute.
She was nowhere.

Yet she is everywhere. Here,
on the road to work
the season breaks open
like a chrysalis, life dissolved,
life begun.

The String Section Skinnydips

After midnight the lopsided Irish moon is heavy
with light and the rocky path to the lake is as clear
as water. The brass players are still drinking
up at the Big House of the Artists' Centre.

The mist fills in the gaps between the hills,
hovers over the far side of the lake and the cellists,
violists, the violinists and bass players strip
to their knickers and beyond and enter the chill waters.

Three writers stand on the shore as still as tree
stumps and watch. Cut off by the edges of a canvas,
the lit greyness would be incomplete,
an environment one could choose to enter or exit,

and that is not the way it is at all.
There are no choices in this complex of factors.
We all have our places and play our parts.
I stand watching the mysteries that

even Yeats could not pin down. The only way
to hold it is in memory, the splatter lap of water
distinct at midnight, the cold air filled with moonlight,
the rocks through my shoes' soles, the slightly drunk poet

standing next to me, the sober conductor
near the water's edge, trying to see the naked girls
through his thick glasses, the mist, the dimness
making him stand very still, concentrating—

like that one second tomorrow before his baton bursts
the music into bloom. Listen. The music has not
yet started to unfold. The violinists are floating,
breasts barely visible. The music is a wrapped satin bud,

waiting, waiting.

Andrew Wyeth's *Distant Thunder*

Her reclining is a woman's reclining
Soft, relaxed,
She lies under her hat, the thunder

Outside the frame, outside this poem
It rumbles and draws
Closer. The half-lidded dog, stirred

Slightly awake, is listening with his
Nose just as the woman
Almost imperceptibly twists grass blades.

The blue is still the backdrop for the tree
Beside her, but the dog is
Alerting and his ears pull the storm closer.

He knows what comes next, his eyes open now,
The puzzle for him
How she does not wake to hear these smells

And taste the cacophony of the world's ending.
She murmurs to his quiet growl.
He moves close and rests his head upon her stomach.

He has his dignity. He will not deign
To skittishness. His eyes
Half close again, but his pupils are black with peril.

Deer Grass

The soft earth imprints your steps from car to paddock
where you see that once again you must hoist
the saddle, sling the bridle across your shoulder,

wind the reins, and heavy-foot the fields to find her
where with only slight resistance she will swallow
the bit, feel the spread of blanket, then the heft

of saddle, the girth tightened. Adjusting the stirrups,
you will smell the leather rich with horse, appropriate
for this hour when although you would rather have propped

the saddle against the damp trunk of the plum tree
only now hinting of bloom, and feel the power of her
as if her muscles were your own, you give in to decorum,

but only this much.
You know already that riding horses is about many things:
the whish of her gait through unmown grass,

jumping small hedge rows with a clean leap,
and compromising between giving up and gaining—
you take her on and she takes you.

How do I know these things when you have told me
only this much: that on a horse you can approach a deer
if you remain as still as caught breath?

I remember the Florida trails heavy with sun and heat,
not your Illinois pasture in this lately arrived spring,
but a time between childhood and now. The flies

I could never outrun, the scrubby land, palmettos,
pines, Japanese cherry bushes lining the barbed-wire
fence, moss dripping from the oaks that occasionally

spanned the road. I'd slow from canter to walk,
lean forward, wrap my arms around the horse's
neck, the coarse mane against my cheek.

But now I imagine you have been drifting
from thought to thought as she takes the lead,
makes decisions at the edges of fields, riding gently

the criss-crossed paths when there in the half sun
of newly leafing trees is the deer's calm stance
containing the stun of injury, dried blood ridging the leg.

She looks across the path at the horse, you, her head
alert for sounds, her nostrils feel the air.
You know the hurt of her and can only sit still,

motionless with desire for healed wounds.
Someday when we have talked the afternoon
into silence, the water suddenly still, I will watch

the horizon, motionless, and you will tell me of the day
you rode to the edge as close as the mare could take you
without giving you away, knowing that to a deer a part

of the saddle is nothing more than a part of the horse,
you carrying the stillness like an extra sense,
I sitting without stirring, as you tell me how

soft the earth was, how the morning opened before you
and the deer stepped into it, as a match scritched
into flame for its few seconds bringing fire to fingers,

closer, closer, then quickly out.

www.ingramcontent.com/pod-product-compliance
Lightning Source LLC
Chambersburg PA
CBHW022119090426
42743CB00008B/915